Gay Adoption

*How to Adopt
as a Same-Sex Couple*

*~ An Essential Guide
to Same Sex Adoption
and Parenting ~*

by Gavin Hsieh

Table of Contents

Introduction

The idea that a family is comprised of a father, mother and a child is not only a narrow view, but also completely disregards the various family structures that have been around through the ages. Are children raised by just one parent, with uncles, aunts, or grandparents, not also living in a family?

Thankfully, society is slowly but surely learning that family is not some idealized structure. Family is wherever there is love and respect between people who may (or not) extend that love by nurturing and raising a child or children.

Same sex couples who desire to raise a child and start a family have been successfully creating loving homes for children over the past decades—through adoption.

There are still people hesitant about adoption in general because common belief dictates that family is defined by blood. But again, this is a false notion. Many individuals who are related by blood end up complete strangers to each other, while there are those who do not share the same DNA but care for each other as if they came from the same womb.

Only you can define your concept of family. Adoption has brought so much joy to couples who have opened their homes and hearts to a child in need of family. As a couple, the bond between you and your partner will grow stronger as you fulfill your responsibilities as parents. And as an individual, having a child will change you in ways that you couldn't have imagined. By loving another person unconditionally, you will mature into a better version of yourself. A child truly is a blessing and everyone who so desires should experience the wonderful joys of being a parent.

If you and your same-sex partner are thinking of adopting a child to complete your family, this guide is for you. Although the process is virtually the same as any other adoption, this book was written with the same-sex couple in mind. You will learn the different ways to adopt a child, as well as get special tips on same-sex parenting and the occasional challenges that you may encounter.

Chapter 1: Getting to Know LGBT Adoption

What is LGBT Adoption?

This is the term used when the adopting parents are members of the gay community. Compared to heterosexual couples, there is not much difference in the process of adoption itself. The glaring difference is that in some nations, LGBT adoption is not considered legal. Even in countries where LGBT adoption is legal, some adoption agencies or institutions openly prohibit or quietly refuse to endorse it.

The Argument about LGBT Adoption

Over the years, different platforms have argued for and against the legality of LGBT adoption. In the United States, many have tried to debate the cessation of such practice. Some organizations asserted that children raised in homosexual families have lower morals and are also prone to a higher risk of abuse. However, this was contested by a number of proponents who pointed out that LGBT adoption upholds the welfare of children by providing homes for children who are in need. The sexual orientation of the parents do not hinder or affect their parenting. Even the American Psychological Association supports LGBT adoption.

Where is LGBT Adoption Legal?

Here is a complete list of countries where LGBT adoption is considered legal (as of May 2015):

Andorra, Argentina, Austria, Belgium, Brazil, some provinces of Canada, Denmark, Finland, France, Greenland, Iceland, Ireland, Israel, Luxembourg, Malta, Netherlands, New Zealand, Norway, South Africa, Spain, Sweden and Uruguay. In the United Kingdom, LGBT adoption is legal in England, Wales, Scotland and Northern Ireland.

Gay adoption is also legal in these parts of Australia: Western Australia, Australian Capital Territory, New South Wales and Tasmania. It is also legal in some parts of Mexico including Mexico City and Coahuila.

While the Supreme Court ruling on same-sex marriage in June 2015, would naturally support the view that same-sex adoption is legal in all jurisdictions of the United States, several questions will no doubt still arise due to other conflicting regulations that could directly affect individual cases. For example, there are states that have limitations on what kind of couples are entitled to adopt, and some states allow even public funded agencies to refuse placement of children with same-sex couples if religious reasons are cited. In the United States, LGBT adoption is currently debated on the national level but as of May 2015 is considered legal in the following states: Alaska, Arizona, Arkansas, California, Colorado, Connecticut, District of Columbia, Delaware, Florida, Guam, Hawaii, Illinois, Idaho, Indiana, Iowa, Kansas, Maine, Maryland, Massachusetts, Minnesota, Missouri, Montana, Nevada, New Hampshire, New Jersey, New Mexico, New York, North Carolina, Oklahoma, Oregon, Pennsylvania, Rhode Island, South Carolina, Utah, Vermont, Virginia, Washington, West Virginia, Wisconsin and Wyoming.

Chapter 2: The Different Methods of Adoption

Domestic Agencies

There are several ways to go about adopting a child, the most common one being through domestic agencies. Upon initial contact with each adoption agency, be sure to inquire as to whether or not they are open to processing LGBT adoptions, because you may occasionally come across a close-minded agency that will be less helpful than others.

In the United States, domestic adoption agencies typically involve the birth mother of the child when searching for the right adoptive parents. Couples who want to adopt a child submit information about themselves to the domestic agency who then passes pertinent information on to the birth mother. The birth mother evaluates the details presented to her and if she is comfortable with the prospective adoptive parents or finds them suitable, the domestic agency facilitates the adoption.

In domestic agencies, most adoptive parents opt for **open adoptions** whereby the adoptive parents get to meet the birth mother during pregnancy. For some cases, they also get to meet the biological father. They form a relationship with the birth mother and maintain communication with her until after the child is born. If you feel that open adoption is the best choice for you, make your preference known to the domestic adoption agency. If not, then inform them that you are considering **closed adoption** whereby all ties with the birth mother are severed after the adoption process is completed. However, closed adoptions are not as popular with agencies and birth mothers so be aware that if you are going for this choice, you may have some difficulty finding an agency that will facilitate it for you.

Independent Adoption

An independent adoption is done without the involvement of an agency. Prospective adoptive parents work with an independent lawyer who aides them in the adoption process. The adoptive parents can either search for a mother willing to give her child up for adoption or their lawyer can look for a birth mother.

This method of adoption gives the adoptive parents freedom over the search process. They can look for a birth mother who specifically meets their preferences. For example, if you want a baby with particular physical characteristics, then an independent adoption will give you the chance to find a birth mother who has the characteristics that you prefer.

Independent adoption has many advantages but you also need to be prepared for its downside. Often, birth mothers change their minds in the middle of the adoption process. This can cost you a lot of money. However, you can avoid this by hiring an experienced lawyer who can help you if ever the situation arises. Likewise, there are some states that consider it illegal for individuals to search for a birth mother on their own. Before you conduct your search, make sure that your state allows it and become familiar with the inherent guidelines and limitations.

Foster Care System

Many, many children under the foster care system are in need of a loving home. This is why the foster care system is also a great method of adoption for you to consider. To adopt a child using this method, contact state agencies who have a listing of children who are open for adoption. They can search their online database for a match. The database includes photographs and profiles of the children so you can evaluate the child before arranging to meet him or her.

Children placed under the foster care system are of varying ages, typically over a year old. Some of them might already be in their teen years. There are also foster children who have disabilities and special conditions. If you want to adopt more than one child, the foster care system is likely the right method for you. There are cases of children who are placed in the system along with their siblings and would prefer to be adopted together. Talk to your partner about your preferences and let the state agency know if you are planning to adopt more than one child.

International Adoption

Adopting a child from a different country is a popular method these days among many couples who wish to adopt. If you are considering this method, approach an adoptive agency that offers international adoption. There are many agencies that facilitate this kind of adoption for you.

An international adoption takes a longer time to process than a regular kind of adoption. Instead of only having to meet the requirements of one country, you need to prepare and prove your intentions to two governments. Prepare yourselves for a lot of paperwork. If you are pursuing this method, it is best to start preparing all your documents ahead of time.

This includes financial statements, bank records and many more.

International adoptions can either be open or closed. Generally, adoptive parents who opt for this method go for closed adoptions. If you choose to go for an open adoption, make your intentions known to the adoptive agency facilitating your adoption so they can negotiate your interests with the birth mother.

Chapter 3: How to Prepare for the Adoption Process

They say there is really no way you can ever fully prepare for parenthood, but you can certainly make the experience less stressful and more joyful by being prepared in some aspects, especially financially. The adoption process, being a bit of a preview to parenting, is also smoother if you are fully prepared. Here are two aspects you want to get right:

Financial Preparation

Adopting a child is a big financial responsibility. Aside from the costs of raising a child, the costs involved in the legal process of adopting one is a big expense. Adoption agencies and birth mothers will require proof of an adoptive parents' financial capability to handle the legal expenses as well as provide for the needs of the child. Considering this, if you are planning to adopt a child, you should be financially prepared. How do you prepare financially? There are several ways to do so, and some of them can take some time.

Seek Stable Employment

If your employment status is not that stable, or if you are unemployed, you and your partner might be rejected as adoptive parents. To ensure your qualification for adoption, you or your partner should have a stable means of income and that may be afforded by employment. If both of you have secure employment, then not only would that be a big advantage in terms of getting approved for adoption, it would also make parenting less stressful Additionally, if one of you is a business owner, that would be a big plus in your application.

Put Aside Money in Savings

This is going to require quite some time if you haven't saved some already. You have to establish a considerable amount of savings before going into the adoption process. You have to prove to the adoption agency and to the birth mother that you can provide for the child. You should not only save enough money for the legal process but also have enough money to show that you can afford to raise the child. For example, your bank account and assets should reflect that you have enough to give the child proper education.

Agencies and birth mothers will also evaluate the flow of money that goes in and out of your bank account. This will give them an idea as to how much money you make each month.

Expenses to Prepare for

Aside from hiring a lawyer or paying the adoption agency fees, there are a lot of expenses that you need to take note of when you are adopting a child. Here are the most basic ones that you need to prepare for:

Prepare for Home Study Fees

A home study is an investigation conducted by an adoption agency to check if the home environment of the adoptive parents is conducive for raising a child. The fee incurred as a result of the home study is to be shouldered by the adoptive parents. This expense is not included in your lawyer's fee or the agency fees. You need to pay the investigator separately.

Prepare for the Birth Mother's and Your Baby's Medical Expenses

If you are adopting a child from a birth mother who is still pregnant, then you have to prepare for her medical expenses. This includes the cost of her delivery as well as her needs post-delivery. Normal birth is, of course, desirable (and less costly) than a C-Section, but it is best to be prepared for any untoward circumstances. There is no telling if your birth mother will need an emergency C-Section.

Your new baby will also have medical expenses. If your baby is healthy at delivery, then your expenses will be considerably lower. However, there are cases when medical complications may arise. Extra preparation will come in handy if ever your little one is going to require additional medical intervention.

Travel Expenses

If you are adopting a child from a foreign country, you have to prepare for the travel expenses. Aside from paying for you and your partners' tickets, you also have to prepare for your child's fare. You also need to prepare a certain amount of money for the processing of her immigration papers. Changing her citizenship might cost a considerable amount so you need to prepare yourselves for this.

Home Study Preparation

Home study is one of the most important parts of the adoption process. Adoption agencies and birth mothers want to ensure that the child's welfare is going to be upheld by the adoptive parents. A home study is conducted by an investigator who visits the adoptive parents' home to make sure that the living environment is conducive for nurturing a child. If you can prove that you have a loving and comfortable home for the child to live in, your chances to get approved for adoption are increased. However, when the investigator is doubtful of your living environment, your chances might be compromised. The investigator can either be a social worker from the adoption agency or from the state. Either way, his judgment is going to be crucial in the adoption process.

Clear Your Legal Records

Most investigators start off a home study by doing a background check on the adoptive parents. He looks into their legal records to search for a history of criminal behavior and child abuse. They will also look into your legal history in general. This is only to ensure the safety of the child. If you have pending cases, make sure that you clear them before pursuing an adoption. Secure all the legal documents that support your claim and present them to the social worker when he conducts his home study.

Prepare Your Home

This is the most important part of the home study. At some point, the social worker will visit your home. Some investigators conduct their home study at a scheduled time while some prefer impromptu visits. In scheduled visits, adoptive parents are given ample time to prepare. They can easily cover up a non-desirable living environment. To ensure that you pass this phase of the home study, you need the cooperation of your partner and other family members in building a good atmosphere in your home. If there are problems that need to be settled between the two of you, better address them before you pursue an adoption. Social workers can sense contention among adoptive parents and this will certainly reflect on their final report.

Fix up your home. Make it neat and safe for a child to live in. Although one normally shouldn't judge a book by its cover, a neat home tends to be interpreted as an indication of a happy home and responsible parents. Before you even start the adoption process, make an honest personal assessment of your home and living environment and complete the necessary adjustments needed, if any.

Secure Necessary Documents

Before finalizing his report, the investigator is going to ask for some documents from the adoptive parents. Typically, social workers require birth and marriage certificates from the couple. They are also going to ask for personal references. Prepare a list of reliable people who can help prove that you are going to be great parents. Examples of these character references can be present or previous employers, a neighbor, a co-worker or a church acquaintance.

Chapter 4: Finding the Right Agency

If you are going to adopt through an adoption agency, you must proceed with your decision mindfully. Adoptive parents typically get all excited with the idea of having a new addition in the family that they jump right away at the most convenient and nearest agency that they find. However, if you act with haste, you may end up unhappy with your choice. Because an adoption is not a trivial matter and it is almost always not quick, you want to work with people who understand you. Finding the right agency is a must. To locate the right agency for you and your partner, consider trying the following ideas:

Look through Online Reviews

Most agencies have websites that you can review. You can read testimonies from previous adoptive parents that they have helped. However, conducting your own independent online search is more reliable. Of course, these domestic adoption agencies are only going to post positive feedbacks given by previous parents. To know how their services truly are, you have to check raw feedbacks from other parents. Search engines come in handy for such investigations. There are also several online forums where adoptive parents exchange ideas. Read threads from these forums or ask for opinions or recommendations from members about adoption agencies they have experience with.

Ask Friends or Relatives for Referrals

Your friends or relatives may know others who have gone through adoption, too. Do not hesitate to ask them for referrals. This is a great way to find a good adoption agency. By considering the first-hand experiences of people who are close to you, you can obtain reliable reviews.

Beware of Fake Agencies

There are a number of fake adoption agencies who have conned excited adoptive parents for money. Because they know that adoptive parents are willing to spend money to adopt, these fake agencies take advantage of their vulnerability. To avoid becoming a victim of a scam, conduct a thorough research before paying an agency. Likewise, once you proceed, make sure that all your transactions are documented well.

Collect and Select

As you conduct a research for the right agency, you will come up with a number of agencies to choose from and this can be very confusing. The best thing to do is to write all of them down on a piece of paper and sit down with your partner to talk about your choices. Weigh the pros and cons of each agency and consider what your partner has to say too. Remember, being parents, you have to work as a duo.

Chapter 5: Establishing a Relationship with the Birth Mother

Whether you are adopting from a domestic or international agency or pursuing an independent adoption, establishing a good relationship with the birth mother is extremely important. In most cases, the birth mother has to choose from a number of adoptive parents. If you have a good relationship with her, your chances of being chosen is higher. Likewise, a good relationship with the birth mother is important when you are considering an open adoption. There are many ways to get into the good graces of your birth mother, but be sure that all of them are genuine. Remember the following tips:

Be Sincere

Before deciding, the birth mother will conduct interviews to get to know the adoptive parents. Most adoptive parents get competitive during this part of the adoptive process. They know that the birth mother will talk to a number of prospective parents for her child and they would love to "win" her over by impressing her during their interview. Do not give in to the pressure. Just be yourselves during the interview. Talk to the birth mother naturally, as you would talk to a friend or a family member. Be open about your sexual orientation. Most importantly, assure her that you can and will take good care of her child.

Some birth mothers prefer to do their interviews by phone but most of them conduct these interviews personally. This is why you should not only prepare yourself emotionally but also physically. There is no need to wear extravagant clothing to show off your financial capability. Just wear decent clothing and observe proper hygiene. Showing the real you will always create a lasting and real impact on anyone.

Be Open to Her Needs

Your birth mother is going to need a lot of support (financially and emotionally) not only when she gives birth to your little one but also after she delivers. Although the arrival of your child is still months away, it is vital to discuss your birth mother's needs. Do not hesitate to ask her about her medical needs. Additionally, discuss the kind of relationship she would like to establish with you and the child. It is best to let the adoption agency and your lawyer mediate your discussion. They can also help in legalizing the terms that you will agree on.

Be Patient

Do not pressure her in any way. Some adoptive couples get too excited and as a result, they tend to take out their anxiety and excitement on the birth mother. No matter how stoked you are, do not stress out the birth mother. Her raging pregnancy hormones and your unbecoming behavior might just cause her to change her mind and this can result in the waste of precious time, money and effort. The birth mother only signs the relinquishment papers 24 to 48 hours after the delivery. These documents will legally terminate her rights as a parent to your little one. Make sure that you are on her good side leading up to the signing of these necessary documents.

Chapter 6: Meeting Your Adoptive Child

This is perhaps the most exciting part of the adoption process for adoptive parents. Meeting the special new addition to your family is going to be an exhilarating experience. Some adoptive parents develop an instant connection with the child. They typically describe it as "love at first sight." Others take a while to warm to the child. Each meeting is unique as each child and family is different. Whatever the outcome is, keep an open mind and above all, an open heart. How and when you are going to meet the child depends on the method of adoption that you are take.

Foster Care System

In adopting a child under the foster care system, it is likely that you will meet him or her in the early stages of the adoption process. Adoptive parents usually browse a database that contains the profiles of children and teens under the foster care system. When they find a child that they would like to adopt, they contact the state agency which then contacts the social worker assigned to the child.

The child's social worker will then determine if you are a good fit. His judgment is going to be based on the documents that you have submitted to the state agency. If he thinks that you and the child are a good fit, he will set several meetings. If you pass the social worker's evaluation, you will receive a placement. This means that the child will be permitted to stay with you in your home for several weeks. The social worker will continue to evaluate you as parents by frequently visiting your home and checking in on the child. Placement is a requirement for children from foster homes before adoption can be approved by the state agency.

International Adoption

If you have chosen to adopt a child from another country, it may take some time for you to meet the child. The adoption agency can provide you with photos and a profile but you can only meet the child that you are adopting in person when you travel to the country where he or she lives. Likewise, your meeting is going to be subject to the foreign country's laws on adoption. Generally, adoptive parents who opt for international adoption travel to the foreign country to meet the child first or to select a child that they would like to adopt. After meeting the child, they go back to their home country to finalize the process. Once the adoption is finalized, they travel back to the foreign country to fetch the child and bring him or her home.

Domestic or Independent Adoption

If the child that you are adopting is still inside the birth mother's womb, you normally need to be at the hospital when the birth mother gives birth. If you would rather not, you can specify it in your terms of agreement too.

Chapter 7: Finalizing the Adoption

You have entered the last stretch of the adoption process. This final step is crucial. You cannot just take the child home without settling the necessary documents first. By legally finalizing your adoption, you are securing custody of the child. He or she then becomes part of your family legally.

Fill Out the Necessary Documents

There are tons of documents that you need to fill out as you finalize your adoption. Some of this paperwork is complicated to understand on your own. If you do not have a lawyer yet, this is a great time to hire one. The paperwork that you are going to fill out is highly essential and must be completed correctly. It is best to fill out the documents with the guidance of an attorney. You have to make sure that you don't make a mistake that could cause you trouble in the long run.

Finalize Your Adoption in Court

This is the final step of the adoption process. You and your partner will be required to attend a court hearing where you will meet with a judge. During the court proceedings, the judge is going to declare that your adoption is approved and is now complete. As adoptive parents, you will be given a certificate of adoption which serves as a temporary birth certificate. You have to hang on to this document while the new birth certificate for your child is being made. This can be slightly different if you are having an infant adoption. In this particular case, the birth mother's presence will be required by the court. She will be asked to sign legal documents that will give you the parental rights to the child.

Conclusion

Same-sex parenting can be complicated. Your child may encounter criticism, hear a lot of questions or comments from other people, or may even suffer discrimination because of it. Be prepared for this scenario and help your child prepare too. There are still some people who look down on gay parenting and there is nothing that you can do to change their opinion. There are only two things that you have control over: how you react to the situation and how you are going to help your child understand what he or she is experiencing. Some children catch on easily and they can stand their own ground. However, there are some children who cannot fully understand and they will need your love and wisdom all the more.

Things can get problematic when the parents are not completely honest with their children. Some parents think that they are "protecting" their children by not explaining their family set-up. Do not hide things from your children. Tell them who you are and make sure that they won't have reason to question your love for them. Afterwards, explain that not all families are the same. Make them see the different family structures of the people around them but make sure that your explanation is also age appropriate. When talking to young children, for example, use illustrated stories to help explain your point. Emphasize that families are built on love and respect.

As much as you would like to protect your child from criticism, child psychologists and experts recommend that you let your child fight his or her own battle. Gay parents who have tried this strategy all agree. Children who can stand their ground grow up to be independent and mature individuals. What you need to do is just be honest with your child, love your child with all your heart and fulfill your responsibilities as a parent. As long as you have raised your child right, there is nothing to worry about.

Being a parent will change your life. Before parenthood, the idea of being a parent might have seemed very far off. But when you become one, you no longer can imagine what your life would be like without your child. This is one of the most exciting (although testing) adventures that you will ever take. Savor every moment of it!

Finally, I'd like to thank you for purchasing this book! If you found it helpful, I'd greatly appreciate it if you'd take a moment to leave a review on Amazon. Thank you!